Lamby's Bre

Story by Jay Dale
Photography by Lindsay Edwards

Rigby®

A Harcourt Achieve Imprint

www.Rigby.com
1-800-531-5015

"Lamby! Lamby!" shouted Erin.

"Where are you?

Here is your breakfast."

Erin went to look
for the little lamb.

Erin looked in the shed.

"Lamby," she said,
"I cannot see you.
Are you in here?"

Erin looked in the bushes.

"Lamby," she said,
"I cannot see you.
Are you in here?"

"Lamby is not in the shed,
and he is not in the bushes,"
said Erin.
"Where is he?"

Baa-baa! Baa-baa!

"Lamby," shouted Erin,

"where are you?

I am looking for you."

"Oh no!" cried Erin.

"Come here to me, Lamby.

Your breakfast

is not in Mom's garden."

"Your breakfast is in here,"
said Erin.